POEMS ON THE LIFE OF THE PROPHET MUHAMMAD

Journeying
Spires and Minarets
April Renga
Selected Ben Nicholson Miniatures (with calligrapher Mick Paine)
Holy Week Sequence
Seven Earth Odes
Mid Atlantic (CD with Graeme Scott)
The Town Boy
Winter Poems

Poems on the Life of the Prophet Muhammad

COMPOSED DURING
RAMADAN AND SHAWWAL 2012

Paul Abdul Wadud Sutherland

MUSLIM ACADEMIC TRUST

First published 1435/2014
by The Muslim Academic Trust
14 St Paul's Road
Cambridge CB1 2EZ
ISBN 978-1-902350-08-0

Reprinted 1442/2021

Designed by Abdallateef Whiteman
Printed in Turkey by Mega Basım

For my granddaughter
Farrah, whom I miss terribly.

For my Muslim brothers and sisters
of Loughborough and especially
Abdur Rahman al-Madani
who are a constant inspiration.

For my dear wife Hajjia Afifa Ematullah
whose love and forgiveness sustain,
and whose editorial acumen has
enhanced these poems.

Contents

I have two sides, one facing the world
and the other Allah

HADITH OF MUHAMMAD

The Rider

He's heeled with no stabbing spurs
who comes across the desert on his Arabian
before he wears his thin Ihram.

And across the whitest wastelands
his horse gallops free, halting at his command
as though reined in by only his love.

Saddle-less it carries him, with a mane
with flanks, that can turn gold, then silver,
combed either by the sun or the moon.

We might be in our graves and far asleep
and still hear its hooves chafing the night sky.

We might be at our labour and go hushed as
horse and master pass by, making our skin tremor.

He once told a youngster riding behind, clinging on
behind, his thin arms round Allah's Beloved,

he once spoke, 'Put your faith in the Lord of Creation,
and fear nothing from death or from life'.

An Unknown

I thought I knew you
trusted merchant
then came the night
when you stepped
into your friend's grave
before his body was lowered
into that emptiness.
You didn't comment
about exact depths
or whether the edges
were straight-spaded.
You lay down
in that messy hole.
I forgot my rituals
and watched you, rest
in another's darkness
unconcerned about
soil marks on your clothes
mud on your turban,
you curled down there
every space of that space
occupied as if the dead
must never be abandoned.
You chanted, hummed
phrases more delicate
than I'd ever heard.
From the coldness
warmth rose.
When you climbed
out, under our torches,
some rushed forward.
I was speechless.
Thought I knew you
but your unknown
was more sweet
than the knowing.

Sayyida Khadijah

The small one passed like a great one through the city
the man some named the orphan
vanishing into our surrounding vista.
A lover of beauty and adventure, like a seeker
from ancient times. He'd judged between the tribes,
found solutions to dangerous disputes, saving
each war-lord's honour, him with little or no position.
I never heard of him quarrelling or demanding redress,
he held his sword like a balance. It was him who was called on
to preserve peace, straighten the easily misaligned.
Discreetly I'd watched him ride out with my camel
caravan and return weeks later with his loads doubled.
I imagined where his sandalled feet carried him; the one whose face
was sketched long ago – flowers in his turban, his radiant youth.
His voice gathered people.
I believed there was passion in his eyes, enough to alter
and I'd been informed that he with few supplies climbed
a near mountain from time to time questing
solitude in a high cave, searching and perhaps praying for
the One God. I knew he was no idol worshipper.
I'd seen the Nur in his gentle expression, his longing to help
whoever called on him; playing with children in a doorway.
Since I dreamt he was the sun, whose light filled Makkah,
I knew I'd have to seek him as my husband.

Sayyida Aisha's Disobeying

The Prophet ﷺ had been instructed by Allah ﷻ to leave his sleeping wife's lap and go and stand among, and pray for, the dead in Medina's necropolis in the middle of night. That was certainty of direction. Imagine the Messenger's sandalled feet pressing into the silted earth as his arms were raised in supplication, in du'a. His high turban's green tail ruffled on his neck as his voice thrilled the ground's deep sleepers. His human weakness called on to uphold the weight of the newly and distantly departed; to intercede for them, a finite being counter-balancing the infinite. Did he intercede, call for each separately remembering an excellent action from their lives or a reason for pity, present them as individuals to Allah? Or did he sweep the deceased up into his heart's arms and ask for their forgiveness as a community to his Lord? His feet aligned with the Ka'ba, he seemed for a time the pole as a human figure around which each world rotated. Maybe sweat glistened like stars on his face. No wonder his wife Aisha secretly followed. Her curiosity stirred her night clothes as she stalked her lord. She wanted to share in the incredible mystery as much as she could. It had touched her when the Prophet lifted his head from her pillowing thigh when Allah Almighty summoned. Did she hear an echo or vibration of that Calling? What had touched her in that sudden vacuum as her master and love slipped away into the night; what pulled her to stand back for the duration – a watcher? She must have her role, even in the vast unknown act of praying for the dead, since her young womanhood had been caressed by Allah's Beloved. She knew she had a hidden right to follow, to risk being disobedient, to show her love could breathe by that vaster love even if she was misunderstood. Such nights she would store up and treasure for her long seclusion after the Prophet's ﷺ death. That night her slender feet orientated towards God's House in Sunnah. She recorded the event passing on to us its wonder. May Allah Most High be pleased with her.

A Muslim Soldier

I watched the sun over hills scorch the rocks
and saw our dream of sudden victory vanish.
Fear moved like a giant scorpion across us.
It seemed terrible shadows grew from the valley
and I remembered loved ones – I'd promised.
Promised to return, would Allah Almighty
will my steps homeward? Who made the mistake?
We huddled around our leader, our commander,
Was it dawn or the dawn of night? I didn't know.
His horse's hooves struck troubling earth,
wanting to carry him off as though a spirit creature
and leave us like stones scattered on the slopes.
I'd lifted my eyes to meet his, if I only could've
come close to our chieftain.

My eyes would've seen a smile, a composed face,
hands controlling the reins, concern beyond anger.
I was enraged at our failure, that God's Messenger
wounded, bleeding, had been exposed by our haste.
I saw my fellow soldiers' fear – he could be taken like
an ordinary man, like a baby's small beginning could
end, in its mother's lap, before it had gulped a breath.
He refused to use his sacred power to crush the enemy.
Risked everything for his faith, prayed that someday
one of those murderers would believe, hold the whole
weight of his conviction, follow in his humble steps;
one who desired to kill him, bury his Islam in the sand.
He raised his hands in a long du'a, called on the One
who gave him strength, knowledge and compassion,
not only to help his friends, but them, his adversaries
to come closer to Allah Almighty who created us all.
When someone questioned his motives, he replied
without reserve, 'I've come as a mercy to the worlds'.

I heard birds, high above, whirring. They seemed
his – not carrying clay-pellets, but they longed for
the battle's dead, for martyrs. I wasn't one of them.
I listened to my faithful wife's voice far away

praying for my safe home-coming.
I inhaled the talking of my comrades,
my Muslims, bright-coloured turban-wearers,
who'd disobeyed. The wind drove the sand
towards us and our enemy's crude words that
our deaths avenged their deaths as if this world
was nothing but revenge and counter-revenge.
My feet ground into earth against a desire to flee.
A sparse Neem tree's inconstant rustle. I heard
my death passing by, calling my name but then ...
Muhammad's strong voice made me believe
I was alive. His praying among retreating
armies, among victors and distressed victims,
his voice perfumed and unashamed of defeat
rose through valleys and gorges towards home
toward bare clouds passing, conferring shade.
His human utterances – his words were more
than speech, more than for us to hear and bear,
his momentous speaking – calling on the Unseen
as if seen and well-acquainted, a friend, a patron,
in that great enterprise that must continue. His
pronouncing at last dominated my heart and fear.

I had no trumpet, but his mouth and tongue, no
drum but human out-pouring, a wise speaking,
a lover's discourse. I weep now to think how
privileged I was to listen to those words – forged
as poetry, burning like the sun through to my insides
filling me with longing to be still, be still and listen
to an intimacy beyond anything I could've imagined
with silence and space, mountain and shadow, leading
to something someone more permanent than the sky
or rock exposed in the light, than red peaks high above.

Water-Carriers

We, Sayyida, his wives and companions,
were water-haulers, our shoulders yoked
for double loads; our anklets ringing we ran
as though frantic goats among raw mountains
tinkling against the whirring clang of swords
and whizzing shafts. We came to the wounded,
dying, mostly unknown, strangers of our faith,
we squatted, our arms grasped their torn-apart
shoulders, we supported their caved-in backs,
held their lolling heads with our hennaed hands.
Those men now nothing more than cloth-dolls.
And we fed them from buckets, ladling with
tilting cups, and forced open heat-blistered lips.
Blood trickled from red eyes; vomit surged
up against our sweet water. We smelt death's
coming and breathed it; became pall-bearers
carrying them back to Medina, to loved ones.
Until from inside our own lungs they seemed
to speak 'I'm dead! I'm dead!' We smothered
had to cry back, 'You're martyred, martyred!
May Allah, The Merciful, bless you. Bless you.'
And then rushed off, desperate to help others ...
by day's end, limbs bruised, our hijabs in rags.

The Teller

I hesitate to write about the blessed man
Muhammad, Allah's blessings and
peace be upon him, but the pen's
in my hand and my heart's moved
and I don't understand what else to do.
I'm no historian, or holy one myself
too stained by craving and the world,
a recorder with some learning behind
and little thought to be scholarly now.
A wiser mind should write of his truth,
relay his excellence, his perfect manners
that touch like breezes filling a slack sail.
I am a sailor who doesn't know the sea;
how can I steer a boat across blank scrolls –
where, then, does this longing come from?
He has entered my life with far more than
pitchers of milk, the quiet saint that disturbed
my playing with toys. He's made my heart beat
differently. I feel compelled to try to follow
his path, that disappears again into mystery,
then changes me once more. No resting
in harbour or oasis. Perhaps I had faith
before but what kind of faith was that?
It seems I knew nothing and now know less;
from where comes my longing to serve?
He has become intimate with me; at will
I might feel him looking over my shoulder.
I wake for night prayers, he's at my side,
I sometimes believe he's deep inside me.
Perhaps he will be when I finish my telling ...
though I might wish to be no more than a tree
that could shade him night and day, a great palm
with waving leaves bearing dates to feed him
when he's hungry. I don't think I'll bear him
children, an inheritance, except these words.
I can't imagine a place in his paradise for me.

The Fast

The outer wooden door's closed
and inner shades pulled down
to deflect the afternoon sun, yet
the heat eats through the walls.

No orchard fruit can be nibbled
from covered bowls, or well water
scooped up from earthen jugs
until the sun falls below the hills.

It is Ramadan, the month of Allah's
greatest forgiving, and of our fasting.
Muslim men and women keep
their gaze and curb their tongues.

In Medina, Muhammad's ﷺ
young wife, Aisha, has collapsed
from the stale air's feverish fire
and he supports her in his arms;

he says, here my Humayra, my
little beauty, suck on my tongue
draw its deep moisture through
your lips to cool your body.

Imagine this honey tongue has
savoured Adam's bitter fruit,
and declared the redeeming laws
that Musa brought from Sinai

imagine it at peace in the mouth
of Dawud when he faced Goliath,
hear it pronounce words of healing
the Son of Mary gave the nations.

Come, my innocent one, and drink
from my skin – a line of liquid love
let it percolate down through your limbs
and keep The All-Forbearing's fast.

Entering Medina

He had unfurled his prayer cloth out across a landscape of no return.
Then rode into the green oasis of Medina, and he let his camel migrate
until it found where it desired to lower its haunches; there he stayed.

Flamboyant chieftains of the tribes paraded the way, wishing he'd
dismount and reside with them; they vied to host the Apostle of Allah
but he allowed a dun creature that had survived the desert to decide.

The one that'd carried him in exile, the wanderer between black tents
Rasulullah honoured and said, you tell me in whose home I should
settle my prayer mat, between whose walls, I should worship my Lord.

I want the grand citizens to know I haven't only come for the rich and
powerful, to win wars, disputes, to conquer empires, but as a mercy
for orphans, disowned, disabled, the poor and for unprotected hearts.

Beast of burden, crossing impossible terrain, who sniffs hidden water,
you without lineage, linked to all creation, carrying light in your eyes
who weeps for a lost foal, say from what root my Umma will grow.

Khadijah's Passing

Blood bonds came to nothing.
All protectors having failed them
except Allah who truly defends.
One loss followed another.
He mourned her in barren land.
The nights of coldness shocked
him and chill winds reminded
of his lost wife and shared affections,
his strongest believer and friend.
The sweet one who never doubted
who lifted the heavy cover off
when he shook in fear of his visions,
who gave up her genteel life, her
jewels and her authority to him,
submitted totally to follow his
steps into the unknown territory
of Allah's Sublimity and Wonder:
that small beginning, where'd it lead?
When his prophethood was too fresh
terrifying and beautiful, and final
as death she was his comforter.

He wished she could have lived,
his first love, dearest of beginnings,
and travelled to the sheltering oasis.

Sayyida Aisha recalls,
A Case of Two Necklaces

You, my beloved, did you doubt me?
Perhaps you had to, because you were
Muhammad, the prophet of a new religion
under the evil eye of factions and gossipers.
Your wife had to be pure as the new moon.
I'd lost my necklace, a wedding gift,
a symbol of love.
I couldn't bear that. I lagged behind your company,
on my knees sieved through silt and dust
for its shiny colours. Its catch had slipped,
weaker than it should've been.
Out there, a young man discovered me.
So determined to find what I'd lost,
at first, I was unaware of his presence.
Had he been sent as a protector? Miraculously
I found the necklace and realised
you and your companions had marched on.
I covered myself with my cloak
and remained secluded and quiet.
You lifted the garment
and the desert sun shone in.
I saw at once your displeasure.
Your kindness, dear husband, a little shaken.
I asked if I could return to my family
until you'd made your decision about me.
You consented with ease. When, finally, you came
to our house you spoke gently and asked questions,
my mum and dad couldn't vouch for me. Suddenly
you trembled, ached and sweated – through you a message …
Allah, the Lord of Destiny, answered
for my innocence.
Gladly you welcomed me back as your wife,
perhaps you also remembered
how important a chain of precious stones
had been to you some time before –
a symbol of love.

The Cave Contemplation

Before elevated to the maqam of prophethood and
revelations tore through him, before Jibreel commanded
him to read and the humble of Allah replied 'I cannot';
at intervals he climbed alone mountain shale, a young

man, to contemplate in a cave. How much did he know?
It hadn't been revealed how to make sajdah or ablution
and yet he had heart to pray and to wash away the 'I'
sensing with certainty the One Eternal would approach.

His ascent up the broken face; he must've stumbled against
beasts, yet continued to seek his way, in mystic absorption
divided fanciful from actual. Who instructed him how, with
submissive courage rising into who can comprehend where?

Imagine starting devotions, and at once you forget everything,
you put on dedicated garments and every time they slip off,
think when you pick up a holy book to read, it turns to ash
or you enter a place of worship and it crumbles to nothing.

He passed through that screen-of-nothingness (across it
no spider had woven) stepped into a cavity of fleeting echoes
and trickling sand; stars looked in, the moon, shadows carved.
Did known creeds nag? Not a Christian, Jew or an idolater –

what inner sense shifted his feet away from religious trading
what unconscious memory gave him the steadfastness to stick
in darkness, believing Light would come, illuminate the walls?
Yet when it did, he was in shock, desperate, at times suicidal.

Consider you come to a high cavern, for one hour contemplate
passing seventy years of worship. How's that ratio measured?
Your heart's stretched, like a line snapped, yet you have faith
to submit and say, I know nothing until You reveal it, My Lord …

The Snake Speaks ...

I desired to see my Creator's best creature, a Mercy for the worlds.

Waited, believing he'd come to my cave for shelter. Then, I heard

him and his companion deep in my chamber, under my jagged roof.

I saw my chance slinking through a low fissure; but his companion

blocked my way with his bare foot. I bit, careful not to use my poison,

hissed my loudest yet he kept his sole fixed. He shook from my fangs'

piercing, his skin wept. Then I listened and heard the Blessed One's

voice, You're in pain, my friend! 'A snake's bitten me. I didn't want to

disturb you'. Rasulullah healed his companion. Let the snake come out.

So I appeared my scales their shiniest. Why have you hurt my friend?

He could've banished me and my kind from existence. His tone implied

he'd hear my story. As Salaamu alaikum wa rahmatullah wa barakatu,

Beloved of my Lord, I wanted to see you, but when I reached the hole,

your companion blocked my way. I bit him hard. I'm sorry I hurt him

but I didn't strike a Muslim with my worst weapon. Best of Creatures

returned Salaams. I, blessed and pacified, in pleasure, curled back into

my hole harmless as a string of beads returning to an old man's pocket.

Irreplaceable

The broken bowl
couldn't be mended
and the delicious food
was wasted. I'd smashed
it in my anger and jealousy.
I was suddenly aggrieved by
my foolishness and asked my
husband, the Messenger of God
what should I do? How to atone?
And he instantly replied, I should
replace both this bowl and this food.
I was left so bewildered by his words
as I had no means to replace the bowl
being not a masterful potter or the food
since I wasn't an expert cook as the one
who'd brought the meal for Muhammad,
– Allah's blessings and peace be upon him.
It was as if my act of violence could never
be atoned. Was that what he meant? Then
if I couldn't precisely substitute the bowl
and its contents for those which were lost
I shouldn't have risked becoming vexed
with anyone or with anything. So, since
everything's uniquely made and exists
it can't be either replaced or re-made
it has a perfect likeness, like each life.
After the incident I was terrified –
to become enraged, as I would not
be able to compensate in his eyes.
I would have to ask forgiveness
of the One who creates everything. The bowl and extra-
ordinary food was all His
not the seductive cook I
was jealous of, not hers
but the Maker's whose
Messenger was my
husband, my love.

The Mosque Builders

We shimmied up the tall palms and cut down with our swords
the fullest, wind-sussling leaves for that first mosque's roof.
As our modest structure took shape we looked up and believed
all in motion was the hand-skills of One Indefatigable Builder

and we built where the palms were spacious as the Milky Way
and utilised their best timber as pillars to support our endless
possibilities – we couldn't gauge what number would come
and find entry, how the mud brick walls would need to expand.

He, the centre and cause of all this, was down there labouring,
the émigré and Prophet from Makkah wrapped in a red shawl –
his arms joined the arms of men thirty years younger than him.
From our leaf-perches we saw the Apostle of Allah as a worker.

When a great palm became a column by which he'd stand and
lead the prayers, some say, they could feel that tree's pleasure.

A Song for the End

If I must lie down under the stars
rest my turban on my camel's neck
let it be between sweet jalil and idhkhir
then I may fall asleep for a thousand years
not wake till the land's greened-over with mercy.

If I must be indoors to keep the fierce
wind out, let it be under a roof of idhkhir
where all the cavities are fragrant with jalil
then a love-scent breeze may take me beyond
wars of this world to a palace of unbroken peace.

If I must lose my footing in the desert
then let it be among those delicate grasses.
I may have no water, yet the sun may not burn
I may lose everything but the love of Muhammad …
Angels send blessings and peace upon him.

If I must fall ill, waste away from fever,
let it be among softness of jalil and idhkhir
then if I twist my body to Makkah or Medina,
east or west the spirit of Muhammad will guide me …
Allah's blessings and peace be upon him.

A Widow Remembers

The water jug may have been low, I heard
the wind chasing leaves. Late
afternoon. Birds chirped. The gate open.
I was at my cooking,
my two young children played in the small yard,
when I saw the Messenger of God
enter. I felt sure my husband
would be soon behind. The Chosen
gave Salaams but hardly spoke
and slipped down quickly to join
my little ones in their game.
They had made a ball out of twine
and were rolling it back and forth.
He joined in, teasing them with snatching
the ball, hiding it behind his back,
 and then returning it to them –
subtly polished or lightened –
he patted them and gave each a hug
and asked them how they were.
I can't remember their response.
I almost laughed to see them
playing on the ground
with that perfect man who had
to be statesman and warrior
who stood up in the mosque
and spoke with poetic elegance
and yet had to fight
many adversaries. Like him
we had all hoped for peace
when we came to Madina.
The best of men was
forced to raise his sword,
now his head was bowed, absorbed
in my children's prattle.
How tenderly the Commander
of the Faithful had once
used his dagger to cut

his cloak around a cat
rather than disturb
its sleeping-place. My children
meowed at the sudden visitor
and new playfriend. I should've
offered him something to quench his thirst
but I didn't think. His clowning around surprised
though I'd heard that he had told
Bedouin tribesmen that they were not of his Umma
if they didn't kiss, hug and play with
their children. Then, again I thought
why hasn't my husband come
and what is al-Amin trying to tell me.
At last, I had to, against my wishes, speak,
'Is this visit pertaining to my husband?'
The Prophet instantly stopped
and lifted his head
as if he had been waiting
and would've gone on waiting
holding back until something inspired
me to ask, as if I'd then be
ready to receive his message.
My children froze in their game
and looked at him. 'Yes'
he said after an unhurried pause,
'he was killed today in battle.'
I don't remember much about
the aftermath but that he kissed
each child on their forehead
and gave me one glance
though I hardly knew he was
in my home any more. A moment
later I heard the gate close
as he left. But the room was left
with Rasulullah's blissful
fragrance lingering
against my growing grief
and fears for the future.
My children, now half orphans,

couldn't return to their frolicking;
they looked up towards me, before they ran
and clung to my side, as if they demanded
something special from me
that seemed also a gift from him.
He didn't need to come
but he came, bringing his blessing,
not that he would alter fate,
but he could and would
out of respect, share distress.
I knew he could perform
miracles but I didn't ask
or expect, it was
that kindly
man's serene
greater humanity
what he gave me
that I preserved
as that day
trailed
away.

Transformation

In forbidden time, after that lusting, light in the sky,
shadows on the wall, my heart confused and repenting,

I had to say it. I had to leave and face Muhammad
who'd given us these laws. Tell him what I had done.

But it was hard. He was a man in power who could
have you killed by a look, a nod to his companions.

I'd heard someone had confessed his act of unlawful
sex and he'd been chased down and stoned to death.

Yet, there he was, I walked up to him, no one stopped
me or demanded what I wanted. He was resting under

a group of waving palms, it was hot, still fasting time.
His friends, resting with him, didn't look like killers.

He saw me and before he could speak I blurted out that
I'd violated his Ramadan, had sex with my wife in daylight.

He looked longer than I'd dreamed possible – maybe
caught my fear. And replied hardly lifting his head, Go

he said, patting my shoulder, buy a poor man a meal –
and by giving be forgiven. I replied, I have no money.

Then just give someone in need some dates. I replied
I have no dates, nothing, I can't even feed my family.

Just then a cart load of the dark fruit was dragged in.
He snatched up a big handful. Here, take these dates

and go back, and give them to your wife and children,
that's enough. His generosity shocked. I walked home.

The Deer, The Bedouin and The Prophet ﷺ

Muhammad, even when he'd gained the status of Prophet and had become the leader of Medina, would travel alone on horseback through the desert night. A mysterious quality surrounded him, an aura, as if he was more connected to the unknown than to the known. He may have visited a distant tribe or been in discussion with the Angel Jibreel. But on this night he was without his companions, returning through immense windless silence. Perhaps it was spring, after a downpour, the ground scented with wildflowers under the 'String of Pearls' and 'Pleiades'. In his youth Muhammad had a reputation for seeing more of the sister stars than most could observe. He heard a strange sound, and perceived through the darkness a black tent of a Bedouin but the sound came from nearby, not from inside. The Prophet, peace be upon him, approached cautiously. Then he saw a white deer, a hind, tethered, near the tent, and heard it crying in anguish. 'Best of creation, Chosen of Allah, please help me'. He dismounted and walked up to the deer tied to a stake. 'O, Habibullah, release me and let me go to my young on the mountain side, let me feed them and I promise by my faith I'll return to this very spot. I must nurture my young and show them how to feed themselves or they'll perish'. The kindhearted man, despite the dangers of infringing the codes of ownership among those war-like tribes, was moved and had to believe. He released the deer that leapt with a flick of her white tail into the night and vanished. Afterwards the Bedouin master who'd been disturbed by the sound of voices came out with his sword raised. He recognised the Prophet of the Arabs and greeted him with respect asking what had happened to his deer. Muhammad explained the creature's sincere request and that he was waiting for her return. The Bedouin preferred to wait too and not make rash decisions when the Blessed of Allah was in his camp. The Bedouin had doubts: how could a creature once enchained, then freed, choose again to be tethered? As this passed through his mind, out of the night came the cry of the deer with the scraping sounds of its hooves. She gave Salaams and said thank you to the Prophet, Allah's blessings and peace be upon him, who returned her Salaams. 'Thank you', the animal repeated, 'now my young will survive'. When the Bedouin heard this conversation he was amazed and touched. He said, 'Please have this special beast as a gift from me'. And the humble of Allah accepted, blessing the Bedouin, and took the white deer in tow, mounted his horse and continued on his way back to Medina. But as soon as he was out of sight and out of hearing, he released her, saying, 'Go, and be with your young, your trustworthiness gives you liberty.' And the sharp-eared creature jumped away a second time into the darkness. Muhammad mused how can a creature that's enslaved, then freed, choose again to be enslaved? Because the One who makes the decisions in the universe may grant that creature greater freedom. He rode on into the silence calling 'Subhanallah, Subhanallah, Subhanallah,' which echoed down the length of the valley from mountain side to mountain side.

An Interlude

From riding into Medina, until his death, he has
but eleven years to secure a kingdom for Islam.

Whose heart and limbs quake to receive the message
who aches and loves so much to receive from Allah?
'I know nothing but what my Lord sends,' he says
laying mud bricks for his mosque one on top of each.

From his entry until his death, he has eleven years
to build a lasting kingdom, a foundation for Islam.

Dimmest ribbons in the east are lightening to pink
believing souls awake and start gathering for Fajr,
and the Belovéd of Allah slips from the embrace
of his red-cheeked love before leading the prayers.

He has eleven years, from his entry to his death,
to love a kingdom and teach the pleasure of Islam.

And young girls play in the dust; they've known
the sorrows of desertion since this world began.
And down, the most courteous of Allah, joins them
although the horns of battle sound not far away.

His entry to his death, he has eleven years
to nurture a kingdom, a safe home for Islam.

He's harried the enemy across the desert plains,
ambushed their caravans and taken their jewels.
He must attack their castles, cut down the proud palms
until each tribe submits, throwing down their arms.

He has eleven years from his entry to his death
to conquer a kingdom, a lasting foothold for Islam.

He's come as mercy. He wishes the people faith,
to reside at peace and share the produce of the land.
But his opponents are sly, they tear up agreements;
they have justified their hate, poisoning his meat.

From his entry to his death he has eleven years
to win a strong kingdom, a calm well for Islam.

How will the new day grow? The wasted land
give fruit? From where will the sweet light come?
Across drifting sands the patient Muhammad comes,
his gracious being surrounds each Bedouin's tent.

From his entry to his death he has eleven years
to give health to the land, and breath to Islam.

He's removed his war-garb to wear a soft turban,
and he calls all the people to the mount of Arafat.
He wishes to speak before he goes to the Sublime
what he says is – 'be kind, to each other ... be kind'.

From his entry to his death he has eleven years
to give a message to the world, a voice to Islam.

Sharing

We shared the same simple vessel when we made our
ablution (it was never broken or chipped). You often
stressed – not to appear too adorned or idle with the rich.
When you poured from that pitcher the stream was crystal.
Your sensitive hand encircled its handle, your ring gleamed
tenderly. I poured for you and its lip shimmered with jewels
as the liquid plummeted. And then plunged for me. What did
you think and feel, my husband, when we shared that tiny oasis
in our home? I can't tell you what I sensed. Let me whisper: my
heart grew quiet and free, jealousies I bore were washed away.
You brought water from al-Suqya, the sweetest you could find.
I gave you the well of love. Sweetest I could find only for you.
Soon, other hands will pour water on my broken body, preparing it for burial at al-Baqi. I'm in panic, my Miftah ul-Jannah,
may your hand grasp one of these skinny fingers as I depart,
softly as you once gripped that vessel's slim handle. I hope
against all my fears to share once more paradise with you.

Seclusion

Muhammad is praying in the courtyard of utter night,
nothing disturbs, preparing for his farewell pilgrimage.
If he sleeps one hour, he awakes, makes ablution and
gives the same weight of time to prayer, before he rests,
he carries his nation and stands facing the Ka'ba, until
his ankles swell, orientates his desire toward that place.
'I have two sides,' he's revealed, 'one facing the world
the other, Allah'. He communes with the unknown: the
farthest stars, white moon, hidden sun, are known to him.
They're elements of The One's creation, Death's another.
He supplicates, submits in sajdah, then stands once more.
In gentle faith in his night seclusion with familiar silence,
he struggles in the way of Allah, struggles inward aiming
past columns and arch-ways of the self to attain the heart.
Time and time again he enters deeper in complete sincerity.
If there's distance – ocean, mountain snows, desert dunes –
there's also furnace of love, yellow amalgam of emotions.
This the true archery – not the outer target but inner peace –
what's loosed into those infinite depths can't be recovered
but by Allah, The Restorer, The Limitless One, The Truth.
He never imagines he's on so excellent terms with the One
that he can neglect Allah. He is Zikrullah, who remembers
before dawn's blush the Creator, His Angels, His Emissaries.
What would this world be like, if he forgot? No one in any
house knows how much they depend on his night prayers.

An Imaginary Eye-Witness

I still can't believe what I saw.
My whole tribe slaughtered,
the long ditch dug and all men beheaded.
I grieve them – why didn't they reckon
that if they had supported
Muhammad, the Quraysh
would've hated them, if they'd stood by
the Quraysh, the Muslims would've
held them in contempt. But they supported
neither so whoever won would be their enemy.
Hedging their fate till the last, till
a ditch was dug for their heads.

I hid on a hillside and watched
till terrified.
                    The night before
I had been in the camp with the men
reciting the Torah. We'd known
exile and survival many times before,
we, the entire Jewish nation,
had seen all we owned destroyed
and had to flee or were taken in chains.
We'd become too cautious, too frightened
to keep faith, yet all that great scroll could say was
keep faith in the One God. I don't understand
how we could've leaned towards idol worshippers
against those proclaiming the Oneness of God.

The torches glowed back the expressions of fear
and trust, my fellow men searching their souls
and the enemy encircling. We'd lived
so long as a people, known the horror of massacre ...
those Muslims fresh-eyed as if there had been
no world before them. We were the old faith,
how could we change, into what? They could dump
our wine skins but couldn't change our hearts. It
was their defeat. We would always stay

Ibrahim's seed, planted in the Judea wilderness,
profound in our faith. It didn't matter if our numbers shrank.
We knew our God had deserted us and stood by
us many times before. Were we not the ones
who had been victorious against the giant of Egypt?
Yet fell to the attack of the Babylonians? – worse
than the idol-worshipping Quraysh, yet God
had given those wreckers the victory.
How our ancestors must have
stared in disbelief, though we had our warners.

My fellow tribesmen looked
bewildered, sensing again desertion.
Ah, those Muslim puppies, didn't know
what us old dogs knew that the day
would come for them too, when their Allah
turns his back and lets their armies crumble
like burnt-through timbers.
Their mothers and wives would scream,
disbelief scribbled across
each warrior's face
as it had cut into ours through that night.
If before, we had recited the Torah
like we did then
we might have been saved. We always
found our best voice too late.

God bless him, Muhammad had been known
to be forgiving, but there was a rumour through
the camp – no clemency – it was the time
for retribution. A last development:
a reprieve, the Messenger had given the verdict
to an old ally of ours – he wanted to be fair to the end.
But didn't he, Sa'd ibn Mu'adh, stick to the trench
and fight beside the Muslims, didn't he warn
us of the possible consequences of treachery?
Still I'd rather have him decide than Umar or Ali.
Didn't the Prophet say, war is deception?
So isn't treachery just another kind of deception,

what was the offence? But we had lost.
He'd freed others, let captives be ransomed, why not us?
We broke our agreement with him
that was the pit of the problem.
And those he'd let go had come
back and fought against him again,
as if he had to kill them three times.
He knew if he permitted us into exile
we'd join with the other northern tribes
of our religion and temperament
and become a bigger force to oppose.
So he had to kill. Yet I'd hoped.
Our treachery was ugly that's what historians
will say –
            and then again I was watching
and listening to the thump, thump
as bodies tumbled into the long trough
as each head was lopped off, each
with its machinations.
Most of my tribesmen went silently
with dignity to their execution, with courage.
But if we had shown that strength
even a few days earlier and joined
the Muslims who we'd signed a contract
of mutual defence with,
they'd have been celebrating our bravery
in the streets of Medina; instead
our women had to wail, our children
become orphans with each sword's
down stroke. Our attitude was too
common, to show courage
when confronted by death, but confronted
by life, we'd rather watch the camel caravans pass
than make honourable decisions,
commit ourselves.
                In the next group
there stepped up my neighbour
to the crudely carved ditch
he had once been generous

bringing food when I was sick;
next a boyhood friend – we'd climbed
the ancient palms to see who could scramble
to the top first. He went down in his woollen cloak –
still a flash of his boyish smile.
I warn future Muslims to do what your Qur'an says
or Allah will throw it back in your face
with the force of Angels.
                              The day was coming
to an end, the last victim neared the trench
torches cast his shadow far across the land.
Thump, his carcass dropped in. I didn't blame
Muhammad, he'd come to give peace
to the warring tribes and we'd welcomed him.
But nothing it seemed was able
to shake our pride, there's the tragedy.
He called us to live in respect
and value our differences
… put away old hates
 through a common cause
renaming the Oasis, Medina
'the City' with its people.
He didn't intend to create an Islamic
State. We gave him no choice.
                              I watched the soldiers
dousing the torches. I couldn't see anymore.
The stench of death faded as I heard
shovels fill the last of the ditch.
My people had been buried.
History won't even know
I existed and from this
vantage point observed.
A wiser man would've run
sought protection
but I stayed to absorb.
That day we had to be content –
that we die and our souls live.

The Human Voice, the Adhan

Bilāl, freed slave companion of Rasulullah, on a platform,
a defenceless elevation, as if a bard reaching in an epic
a stunning, heroic episode, lifts his voice, towards the
still visible stars as he calls the people to worship Allah.

Yet there can be no force in that addressing, no coercion.
A humane speaking, eloquent, with so many modulations
was what the Blessed Prophet, Faseeh ul-Lisaan, selected
to summon the citizens to their prayers in the new mosque

and to praise al-Rahman. The clear voice, quivering, rising
into last nocturnal shades, first tints of dawn, reaches the ears
of a young nation; this throat instrument, that has its birth
and its death, its pain and joy, after the war cries have faded

into the immediate past, before hubbub of the city, Medina …
that fragile organ which a released arrow can silence at once,
that sound resembling a parent calling their children home,
that can echo a widow's grief yet is unique to each person,

that humble oracle awakes the sleepers; stirs the warriors,
wayfarers, householders to the true Jihad, the task, the love,
to serve One God, and Muhammad His Messenger, to be
loyal, to alter the human heart and make it pleasing to Allah.

In that singledom of one voice, its mystic trembling charms
creation and unrepeatable tones give reverence to the Creator.
Bil l has stepped down, yet his uttering expands into space
as if human destiny, its beginning and end, was in each Adhan.

Saahib ul-Miraj

Best of Creation, the Seal of Prophets,
climbed the sky where there was no sky
on the warm saddle-less back of a Buraq –
why should it not have had a human face
who carried the dedicatee of humanity?

On Jerusalem's angelic Temple Mount
he greeted the prophets, leading them in
devotion to the One, aligning traditions,
and then rose on the joy-weeping Buraq
to where his escort, Jibreel said, 'Sayyid

I can go no farther, only human beings,
once perfected through that Holy Light,
can approach that unapproachable Light.
But you, Mustafa, have permission to
go nearer, to intercede for humankind.'

What celestial fields did he pass through
that cannot be named fields, to approach
a throne more expansive than the universe?
How did his simple heart muscles remain
beating, how did his lungs digest that air?

He mounted the creature of unending faith.
And sometime in a cave, the world invading,
Muhammad passed on that light and beauty,
his heart's whole mercy-load, to his closest
dearest Abu Bakr As-Siddiq, to be threaded –

like a sun-ray through clouds – through saintly
masters in each generation from every culture.
Somewhere in paradise a Buraq paws unseen
pasture, in pleasure weeps to recall his ascent
to the seventh heaven and his blessed rider.

Sayyida Hafsa

One day Aisha and I were eating
together, delicious food already on our plates.
I knew Aisha was displeased
with me sharing with her and our husband.
Muhammad, may Allah's
blessings and peace be with him,
at that moment
walked into where we sat on the floor
and recognised the tensions
in a soundless rapid gesture
like a miracle worker
he took up my plate with one hand
and Aisha's in the other
and gave hers to me and mine to her,
and said, 'What's hers is yours
and what's yours is hers.'
I had to admit he was addressing Aisha.
This exchange silenced us both.
Perhaps I wanted him for myself.
But hers tasted as good as I imagined
mine would have tasted.
But Aisha didn't look like
she was enjoying my food.
My opponent was particularly
crushed, because she considered
herself the best, for ten different reasons
she liked to state.

I felt an outsider
perhaps too much a Quraysh
though my father was a key companion.
The Messenger of God divorced me
and needed to be told by Jibreel
that I prayed at night and fasted, was righteous.
He took me back and treated me
like his other wives, showing
affection, as he had once

accepted Aisha's innocence
from divine revelation.
Some rumoured that his messages
were wish-fulfilling. He wanted to divorce
me, and was ordered 'no': how could that
be a sign of self-gratifying?
Maybe there was a subtle rift.
I offered him a honey drink
which he deeply enjoyed,
but he only welcomed it once
on one visit, I imagined
the trickery of the other wives
had somehow put him off.
I gave him my learning
wanted to relate the genius of his actions
to future believers. At times
we wives were like birds twittering
around him, but he had a way –
a turn of phrase, a changing expression –
to cut through squabbles,
a manner of altering a petty event
in a second to reveal something more.

I felt the incident with the food
was a message, reminding us
that we owned nothing here,
that everything belonged to the Creator
and there was never anything
to be possessive about
because nothing could be possessed
as we would all have to learn
again and again. In the end
we would value every second
with the Chosen of Allah –
his sweet breath
his wonderful perfume
his love of us –
we could never
value or thank him enough.

Water and Wine and Milk

On the Prophet's ﷺ Isra and Miraj at one point
he was offered these substances to drink.

He could have chosen water, easily,
fluid that rescues the thirsty camel,
the substance that washes the body
that brings nourishment to orchard
and fields, that ripens the barley and
signals with a few dates the opening
of the fast, the element that falls from
the clouds and makes the wadi gleam
sweeping off the desert grime like rust
and lets the scented wildflowers spring
from the land; water ritualised in wudu
to prepare the faithful before prayer.

He could have grasped the wine, though
forbidden, how can it be unlawful when
your Lord offers it as red as a favourite
wife's cheeks, blushing as though dawn
with mysterious early light, or twilight's
afterglow, marking beginnings and ends?
Wine, sacred, with its intoxicating flames
that the heart feels in deep love, longing
for its Lord's embrace. Fire that rushes
through a warrior's limbs as he prepares
to confront death. And passion that wins
over fear that gives a taste of paradise.

He chose milk with which she-camels
suckle their calves, and yet is given on
in rich generous streams to nurture men.
Milk, that nourishes the young in ways
no water can, the white substance that
calms fire that can destroy in its excess;
the gift that shows a husband's wish for
forgiveness before he approaches and
makes love with his wife; the creamy
pool that suggests purity, the promise
to please and be at peace, that soothes
the cries of the newly born, as if a new faith.

Patches of Compassion

'Don't throw out any garment until you've patched it,'
the Messenger of Allah remarked. Perhaps, he implied
more than fabric ruffed in the wind on his wayfaring back
as he searched through a dust cloud with a rider' provisions –
Deneb and Altair vanished like children under a sweaty khamisa
or when he gave his cloak as an undercloth for his daughter's body;
they'd washed her five times with strokes of lotus leaves, and had
nothing to wrap her in, to be a soft veil between her and the earth
or when he cut his turban folds to be a head-covering for a slave-
girl who had reached puberty and now trembled in a dim corner,
him diminishing his symbol of power to comfort her delicacy.
Did he mean – forgive human beings, keep patching relations,
preserve long what you have? If, you stay with mercy, who
knows when an old tatty coat will become saintly apparel?

Abd-Allah Ibn Umm Maktum

He knew I could speak what
I couldn't see when he asked me
to call his Umma to prayer (taking
my hand, leading me to the exact spot).
Could speak more beautifully because I
couldn't watch the words rise from my lips
and doubt their wonder. Better not to be able
to inspect when addressing, as if I was in touch
with the Eternal. I required a sense in darkness,
listening and feeling, by vibrations of language,
the Shahada. He, the kind, Khateeb ul-Umam,
realised the strength in my flaw. He recognised
behind a vacant stare there existed store-rooms
of secrets, the way he spoke of orphans and the
disinherited as if they were connected to something far bigger and truer than blood relations.
At times he quietly echoed, hummed my words.
He'd spoken, 'In this world I see myself a wayfarer, who barely belongs.' Naturally he saw
how these eyes that concealed could give
more intensity to a tongue to tremble it
with love for the One, my Cherisher,
who gave me breath but not sight.
And I sensed that the Messenger
in drawing me from my void
to use my voice to summon
was saying: be grateful for
what Allah gives, for what
He seizes and gives again.

Sayyida Aisha

When the love of my life died
I was seventeen.
He'd founded an Islamic nation,
shattered the weapons
of the aggressive tribes,
made the high palms
bow to kiss the sandals of a wayfarer
transformed thieves into scholars
given us the right manners
for every action,
had conquered Makkah
and made it possible for us to visit
our families there,
he'd emptied the Ka'ba of idols
written letters to emperors
made safe the routes across Arabia
brought the beautiful language
of the Qur'an into our
everyday rooms and places of worship,
given protection
to every new born daughter,
changed the status
of the poor and orphaned,
the blind and unprotected,
he'd opened a passage
for us to go unhindered
on Hajj, to perform the rites
specified, without fear of attack,
he'd set humour above anger,
made the oppressors hide
behind closed doors and beg for mercy,
taught us how to be kind
and forgiving,
given us a store of remedies
to heal the sick, to comfort the dying,
brought sacredness into every dwelling,
converted the most stubborn leaders,

taught us how to worship the One God
please and remember him
through prescribed prayers, fasting and
peaceful service,
he'd changed the heart of murderers,
given power to the weak,
rights to the slave and captive,
shone light into dark superstitions
secured wells from which everyone could drink,
he'd defeated the boastful
and set a limit on magic
he'd performed miracles
so we would know there is nothing
Allah can't achieve,
he'd shown us how a strong leader
could be humble and stoop to play with children,
made the lost youngsters
on the street feel cared-for,
established the power of charity
taught fathers how to be fathers
mothers how to be mothers
revealed the reality
of mercy and how it could
transform the human heart,
he'd left us precious gifts
that we stumble on with surprise
everyday,
shown how being trustworthy,
honest, defeats any trickery,
he'd disclosed that there are rewards
that can't be seen,
he'd given the dying hope
made paradise
a believable goal,
he'd challenged death
and taught us that
being a human being
was the most favoured rank ...
I lived forty-nine years
in my widowhood.

The Qur'an

Like desert songs, its recited verses gathered-in the red-scarved
camel driver, the safflower-dressed buyer in the marketplace;
a turbaned trader, by his leather goods, heard its undertones,
a veiled woman playing with her infant squealing on her knee,
a poor servant on an errand pricked her ears. It was their speech
as much as Rasulullah's. They understood each Sura's rhythm
its colloquial elegance, in calls of a traveller, in shouts of the
weigher of measures, the words measured to their own meaning
that frightened and soothed, that had to disturb. The city had to
listen to its birth and death, the sweeping-away of empires.

Yet who spoke it, freeing an utterance past the timbre of heroes,
whispered of Infinite Nur, the Vast Shaper, the Lord of Destiny
whose language resounded in lightning's crack, in a flash flood's
mud-churning roar, in a taciturn moon suspended between stars.
It came divinely formed, sweetly intense asserting the unseen and
inaudible in the Name of the Most Compassionate and Merciful.
Inspired Muhammad sweated, like a writer striving for a phrase
a calligrapher with his soot-ink nib seeking the best letter-shape.
He knew words were surface to a more sublime reading, an ocean.
And the safflower-dressed and scarlet-scarved heard that too.

Maybe A Slave Girl

When his wives were dissatisfied
and wanted more hours
or to receive gifts, though I hardly
saw him, I was grateful
to be under his roof,
the one they called
The Messenger of God, Rasulullah.
I would stroke his green turban cloth
down both sides of my face
and across the top of my head;
the piece he had given me to be my hijab
at puberty. I expect nothing –
why should my feelings
count for anything?
am I not a slave? But when
I hid because of my bleeding
he recognised those emotions
and fears and immediately acted.
I was frightened to trouble anyone.
I remember seeing his hands rising
to unravel a loop, then the knife
moving towards the scented cloth
and hearing it tearing
I almost felt for the material
as a piece was separated then given to his wife
who handed it to me and I quickly looped it
over my hair.

I often saw him and but only once thanked
him for the gift, and he said,
'I'm a slave too, a slave of Allah.'

I cleaned the water jug in a stone
alcove, quite shallow. I went into
his room and saw his
spread palm leaves as a bed
and at the head a leather cushion

with a leather thong stitched in and
out through the hide.
I swept off the dust,
and attempted to puff it up
make it more comfortable
but the stubborn brown bag
remained flat. With a besom
I chased the persistent refined grit
and washed utensils diligently
considering any contact
with what he'd handled
a mysterious blessing.
'Be jealous of me'
I sometimes said under-breath.
If they had known
how much I thought of him
they would've been more than
envious. I tried to spruce up –
his palm leaf matting too.
He, who deserved to repose
under silk covers, slept
in a near-unfurnitured room,
only a herd animal's skin
to relax his head.
Now and then his wonderful
fragrance filled the house
and I bathed in his perfume.

I recall how he put human
needs above a precious thing
as precious as his turban.
Like him, I had no desire
to be free.

The Prophet ﷺ and a Child

One day, you asked a child 'how are you?' and heard
of his distress, which you half-guessed by his eyes.
His pet bird had died and the boy was in mourning
for that timorous being who'd chirped and quivered
through the household and had become a close friend.
You (May Allah's blessings and peace be upon you)
shifted your attention from duties and adult dialogue
to that tearful child. 'What did you call the creature?'
you asked in respect. Everything must be named as
if that minor was another Adam in his little paradise,
now invaded by grief. The boy replied it was a secret.
You, Habibullah smiled giving out a mellow chuckle.
The toddler grinned to possess a secret on a Prophet.
Under his arms you lifted him up on your knees and
hugged him and unravelled how it was in this world –
that the bird's fate was ours and, of course, your fate.

Entering Makkah

We marched into Makkah, then to the Ka'ba,
the violence of the Quraysh was subdued,
they stayed behind closed doors
and asked for reconciliation
and Allah, through his Prophet,
was forgiving. We heard the Adhan
from above Abraham's black stone,
our horse trappings and armour shone but not with
the moon-glow of
Muhammad when he entered the shrine
and stared at each idol – the stone, the wooden,
the tall, the short, the crude, the well-carved fell down
on its face before his staff and his gaze.
The key was turned in the lock and he entered the Ka'ba
prayerfully he stepped over its threshold.
He had every idolatrous image erased from the walls
except the Virgin and son, and a picture
of Abraham. The finery of his understanding,
who could grasp? He was Allah's Elected,
his every action was just and generous.
We watched in amazement
and saw families, once parted in great hostility,
joined in a greater harmony,
all past offences pardoned and we wondered
at the power of Allah who could bring about
a triumph and in the next moment
accomplish a true truce.
We rejoiced that day, more than any other
since we didn't need to
shed blood or see our comrades wounded
or dying, our opponents' homes in ruins
and their wives and children distraught;
that day we quickly went from battle
to peace and to worshipping al-Salaam.
We heard the hollow resound with Allahu Akbar
and we believed the time of fear was at an end.
There was no war booty, except

that people relinquished their trust
in idols and turned to the One God.

I will sleep tonight in my father's house,
or under a tented sky. I'll embrace and guide him
towards the gentle light of truth. And he will
rejoice when it touches his eyes. There can be
no darkness after this day; everything is joined
in the brilliance of Allah – the Most Compassionate
and Merciful. Rejoice, Makkah, for your streets
will be free from strife and your children
will have nothing to fear; no cruelty
can survive in the place that al-Kareem has blessed.

I'll sit in my father's company
and gather my family around me; we'll share
the best food of concord and forgiveness
we will share in the dawn prayer
and lower our heads in sajdah
and give thanks to Allah
before the rising of a new sun.
The ancient green palms will rustle
in a new breeze; the grounds
of torture will be calmed.
Those forgotten will be remembered,
the hero will be a man of benevolence.
The faithful will be rewarded.
My heart has felt the Prophet's love
and I yearn to extend it to my loved ones
to all who acknowledge there's no God but God
and Muhammad is His Messenger.
Those who couldn't make their Shahada
we'll give them time. That day contained no force.
Who asked for protection received it.
The future will not believe that
such a day of Grace ever occurred
but we saw it and were startled
to look over the empty, silent city
before us, the brutal marketplace

without slave-traders stood unassuming.
That day they all covered their heads.
We observed Makkah's lavish leaders
wearing modest clothes, under veils
or without armour, presenting themselves
to the Commander of the Faithful
asking pardon, and going away
without fear of reprisal.
The future will never believe that
such a time of reconciliation
could happen on the earth
in our desert land. But we saw it
and marvel still.

Abu Quhāfah (father of Abu Bakr Siddiq)

I didn't know why I should've been allowed
to live, so long, except to witness my son
return, with an army re-enter the city.

I asked my daughter, as the early sun
drew sweat and many insects droned,
to guide me up a near valley mountain.

With her help and my staff as supports
I zigzagged between coarse boulders,
climbing the scree until reaching a point

that overlooked the hollow of Makkah.
I asked her to describe what transpired
because I could no longer see for myself.

I felt my seventy years leaning on my stick;
last night's coolness long having withdrawn
a breeze was already stirring from the south.

As if celebrating, in the air, songbirds chirped.
I was reminded of my youth when I climbed
up here and observed thousands on the wing

a black mist of small birds speeding against
an invincible army that marched on the Ka'ba.
I saw that force decimated; soldiers fleeing.

Then she spoke, telling me of black massing
Muslim troops, moving in different streams
towards the city; she reported no resistance.

I was relieved. The Quraysh had capitulated.
There would be no need for a second massacre
of those daring to oppose the Will of Allah.

I said to my daughter, let's go home, quickly,
I felt her arms surround my chest and take more
than half the weight of our jarring descent.

And Mountains Didn't Move

On his mule, Duldul, the Prophet Muhammad returns

from trying to convert the tribe in a mountain enclave.

He hasn't succeeded – using his experience, faith, skills

– Surahs of the Qur'an with their promises and warnings –

to convince the stubborn tribesmen, that there is only

 One God to worship. They still cling to ancient idols.

He slumps on his mule homewards; his thoughts grow

grim, reliving that population's arrogant name-calling,

he feels depressed that he was able to achieve nothing.

In the best generation of Muslims, he couldn't persuade

the backward adherents to accept all the Light has shown

is noble, courteous and beautiful. He mourns his failure.

His sorrow has inspired Allah Almighty to summon Jibreel

to go to the Seal of Prophets telling him he has permission

to command the Jinn of those mountains to hurl themselves

down on that people, burying them under rock and rubble.

'No', he replies to Jibreel, 'I won't have the peaks thrown

down on obstinate humans. Instead, I'll pray that someday

one of their descendents will follow my way to Allah al-Haq'.

Faithfulness

In your Mosque, you and your companion-family
welcome sixty Christian followers from Najrān.
You, Best of Creation, wear an exuberant cloak
and under it you draw your dearest and most loyal
around you, Fatimah and her two sons and Ali.
For each belief, as the revelation pronounced
'For each we have appointed a law and a path.'
Not you, under the widest cloak, or your visitors
desire to press religious differences to cursings,
the group leaves with a treaty respecting their faith.

You calm differences sharing what we don't know.
You, Chosen of Allah, honour those who pursue
their sacred work, who are sincere in their searching,
those are the true strangers, 'those ready to depart'.
You know hearts can only be altered through Allah's
intervention, no force or plotting would bring nations
to your way. The revelation has declared, 'And if God
had wished He could have made you one people.' But
the Most High gives split routes to follow; and yet His
ways are many as all the breaths since creation began.

Faith that counts comes from more than knowing
and every dispute must tend to an over-reacting.
We need to vie, by determining on good actions
to impress our Creator, not on wars or conflict,
but revealed to you, Muhammad, saying, 'Unto
God you all will be brought back and He will
inform of those matters in which you differed.'
Knowledge cannot split open what God intends
to conceal, His design, yet the firm intention to do
caring loving acts brings us into closeness with Him.

Canonical Prayers

You recognised your end was near, when Jibreel
recited the Qur'an twice to you in the same year.

You, perfect man, truest creature from beginning,
had to die and suffer like us – being human.

You cried out, 'O Allah, help us mortals, as we
go through the agony of dying.' You left much

for us to live for, the prescribed prayers, so when
we bow our heads and sink to our knees, bringing

our foreheads down to touch to kiss mother earth
to submit to Allah when we pray, as you informed

you surrender with us, and us with you in Sunnah.
And yet there was much to be fulfilled before your

earthly end; time was expanded for you to achieve
what needed to be done. Allah, The Beloved, is over

time and space. The dimensions are slaves of Allah
and that One gave you grace. In truth you exist more,

blessed Naasir, most honoured in the divine presence,
Muhammad in spirit as we are when the body's shed.

You gave us, Salawaats, greetings of praise and peace
for you, prized above by the Cherisher of the worlds,

a prayer sayable in the reek of battle, on beds of passion,
from the blackest cell's mouth, from the crudest sinner,

because that One's Mercy and Love can't be curtailed
by anything or by anyone that exists in time and space.

Fruit of Charity

You gathered in baskets, an alien and beautiful fruit ...
no matter how delicious and juicy the enclosed pulp,
how colourful, textured and sweet-smelling the skin,
that fruit grew; from the core of forgiving, from that
stone, roughened or smooth, oblong or round, swelled
the taste, the fruit, of charity. You offered soft harvest
again and again, from orchards beyond dizzy orchards,
offering the best land, that can't be inherited by family
or tribe that rests under the sun to provide for the needy.
You taught that lush fruit matures from the discipline of
forgiving those others who opposing our acts of kindness
throw the fruit back in our face. You showed your Sahaba,
a dweller of paradise was a pardoner of those who hurt him
every day, before sleep, confirming Allah was the source.
That Greatest One had revealed, 'that he would use some
of you to test others of you'. You knew stone's sharpness
when you forgave the killer of your beloved uncle Hamza,
when you listened patiently to the crazed ramblings of Hind.
Did you really believe that she who despised you could now
love you? Or did you have to suck dry the stone of forgiving?
But what does love count for without the capacity to let go?
Strange: humility to bear Allah's decrees can generate love.
You'd put the extreme personal aside, pleasure of revenge,
for something else, for what will be honoured to this day.
You said to the Sahaba, 'Love each other'; they looked
satisfied to love each other in a family, in companionship.
But you came back: 'You'll never carry the weight of my
faith, till you love everyone'. They appeared puzzled by
love's weight, curse, and joy, by the Allah of your Allah.

Ramadan, month of the Fast

Light's first hint emerges and the fast starts
and when the sun has gone, it breaks and we
eat and drink again in no continuous denying.
But, for a time-frame, connected to the moon
and varying year to year, for an episode of days,
we waive, suspend, our rights to nourishment
for another manner of nourishing and of being.

You, Mustafa, dedicate this yearly abstaining
as an essential act to please the All-Forbearing.
In that emptying, a new substantiating occurs.

What can that substance be but that the soul,
given time and space, breathes and flourishes
against the ego, compelling it to step back and
allow the mystical substance of truth to enter?

These truth-steps are subtle, hardly discernible
that can be stamped on the heart and tooled
into the mind till more than understandable.

You know fasting renews our pleasure for what
the senses receive, but also inspires us towards
what the senses fail to perceive, and yet exists.

The world can only revolve so far towards its
own un-worlding, something else must enter to
assist the process, to disturb material existence.

Life can only advance so far towards its death.
Something must break in to demand we observe
our dying before dying, our loud I's shrinking
as if our desires may decline during Ramadan
and physicality diminish to allow for a gradual
expanding that can't be measured by days or weeks
that is real as food displayed on a floor's tablecloth.

You, Messenger of Allah, understand how the
I's dwindling illuminates the soul and polishes
the heart's looking-glass. Through Ramadan's
sanctions, you give to each Muslim the occasion
to displace the egoistical, for spiritual sensitivity,
a taste of saintliness in the limits of every-day.

We touch and feel what your wonderful enslave-
ment to Allah, the Nourisher, implies – a blissful
tenderness, a pleasing love that feeds the nervous
misguided I, more than that I can nourish itself.

The Whisperers are muffled and baffled during
our intent to abstain, and the air we take in, clears –
is more open to communications from our Lord.
Everything might alter through that dismissing
of our 'craving enjoyments' for the prospect
of pleasures far less perceivable and more true.

You, teacher and guide, stay in seclusion the last
ten days of that interval to intensify that silencing
as though you are again in the cave; each Ramadan –
restoring what so easily can be covered with dust.

You, Najiullah, restrain earthly pursuits, in patient
quietude, respectful, attend during the night prayers –
between the fast before and the fast to come – listen
to the voice you heard, in darkness, the Compeller's.

You affirm for us, a time, a space in time, when
we can recognise beyond the absence of food
and drink, a superior disappearance, a vanishing
of all wrongful desires, our pride and selfishness.

You prescribe a hearing, a taste, a chance to gaze
at Allah's gifts of forgiveness and spiritual delight,
the hope of watching destiny's new moon appear.

Pilgrimage to the House

'Gently, gently! In quietness of soul! And let the strong
among you have a care for the weak.' Muhammad 圖..

Your pilgrimage is not a journey to a particular place
at a particular time, though it is that; but it is a state
of being where the mind must spend its night hours
in the desert under the radiant moon if we are lucky
and where before, the peaceful, since nothing can be
harmed, stand on the Mount of Mercy in supplication
remembering Abraham's legacy remembering Adam's.
All must be connected and renewed, the ancient and

the immediate embraced through the prescribed ritual.
You, Khaleel-ur-Rahman, friend of the Compassionate,
led your people, on your farewell pilgrimage, giving a last
example of manners, the purpose of Ihram, of procedures.
But how I wish to know what was in your heart, at each point
of praise when you lifted your hands in reverence, or selected
the pebbles to stone Shaytan, what shook you when you stood
gave your short address on the Mount of Mercy – thousands

listening – what trembled through you at the last revelation?
All is too gentle to know; in the journey the general slips off
to an intimacy. The pilgrim steps into that silence again and
again, in a gathering of the countless and yet tenderly alone.
There too, in the state of purity, comes the moment to help
others in greater need wherever or whoever Allah reveals
as though this sacred undertaking was a symbol of another
Hajj whose measuring footsteps are over a lifetime at least.

Blessed are those who walk in that way, with you, if their feet
ache or can not walk, but move from a gentleness to a deeper
gentleness, from caring to a more caring, from being kind to
a higher kindness, a love imaginable to a love unimaginable.
Blessed are those who step with you, honoured Siraatullah,
path of Allah, Muhammad, blessings and peace be upon you,
cherish those who step through the veils of birth and of death,
with you. Without fear they come to the House without grieving.

Death of the Prophet Muhammad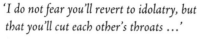

'I do not fear you'll revert to idolatry, but
that you'll cut each other's throats …'
—THE APOSTLE OF ALLAH

I remember those words … predicting violence against
the intimacy of illness, of love, against a hijab's delicate veiling.
That was the outer world. Inside, words had little impact
seeing that blessed human being in agony,
feeling the light vanishing. Against the darkness
we had to ask a neighbour for oil to light the room's lamp,
the Chosen of Allah lived so simply, as if the room
was in permanent sajdah, though no-one wanted to see
his passing in severe pain. He never said
a prophet would depart peacefully.
He rose from his leather pillow time to time
requesting liquid to temper his fever.
I tried to imagine his sensibilities
that could feel in his veins the poison
that had tried to kill him three years before.
It was hard to accept that he needed us, who a few
months earlier looked destined to live many years, who had
the power of multitudes to call on.

Perhaps there should've been more of us present.

We were a small family joined in grief, each wishing
to pour and pat cooling water on his brow, on his head.
Watching the well-spring of our lives in anguish
we forgot our quarrels –
about who was the best, who our fathers were.
Comments passed into the unknown, wishes and pleadings
obscured by our urgency, us wanting to redeem
mis-stated phrases or gestures that seemed relevant
but against imminent death were burdensome. We wished
to throw off everything that might harm.
This need became too selfish
and we longed to know what the hidden significance
of this moment might be, but its dear messenger
was in mist and becoming silent.

Someone said, I wish I could be in your place.
We didn't believe their desire to take on his suffering
but he did, and glowed suddenly
in quiet knowing and found voice
to praise the speaker.
We couldn't feel jealousy either.
The lamp burned in the darkness
as if we were in a cave, a womb,
what was going on outside lost its meaning.
He gazed at one of us using a tooth stick,
sensing Muhammad's need, that friend took
his miswak and passed the softened root over to the Prophet –
it went from the mouth of a Sahabi to the mouth of Mehboobullah,
almost a last gesture, a final cleaning; he found energy
for a fraction more, what Allah granted us.
Why had there been a sight of recovery
only to have him taken
before the next moonrise? He sweated so much
and when he could no longer speak, each shiny
drop on his forehead on his clothes was another act
of asking pardon for his Umma.
Some say his drenched garment was handed on,
became a healing relic to inspire devotion;
others refuse to believe such things.
After Rasulullah's death the legends
crowded in as rapidly as disputes
about who should lead the Muslim nation, be its Khalifah.

I was in the room with that loving human
who breathed with us, the Messenger of God
of everything we cherished, who had transformed us,
and left us that cool dark evening, speechless,
the lamp oil depleting.

He was buried where he died.
The rest must be left ...
the All Forbearing, the All-Cognisant,
Allah knows the truth of what followed.
It is in Him we put our trust. ﷺ